Roc

A Guide and Inspiration for Creating and Designing Your First Rock Garden

By

Karen Elliot

Copyright © 2015 by Saxonberg Associates

All rights reserved

Published by

BookSumo, a division of Saxonberg Associates

http://www.booksumo.com/

Join the VIP Reader List and Get...

Send the Book!

Join my private mailing list of readers and get a copy of my book: ***Garden Ideas: An Introduction to Different Gardening Types and Methods*** for **FREE*!*

In this book I introduce many of the gardening methods you've heard of, but may not fully understand. We will discuss: *container gardening, lasagna gardening, heirloom organic gardens, water gardening, bonsai's, straw bale gardening, and others!*

Learn about the different gardening methods available! This book is not available anywhere else and is only for my private list of readers!

You will also receive updates about all my new books when they are free. So please show your support.

Also don't forget to like and subscribe on the social networks. I love meeting my readers. Links to all my profiles are below so please click and connect :)

Facebook

Twitter

Google +

ABOUT THE AUTHOR.

Karen Elliot handles all of BookSumo's home and gardening topics. Karen is an avid gardener and lover of the outdoors. Her first book: *Fairy Gardening: A Complete Guide to Creating Beautiful Fairy and Indoor Gardens* was an instant hit with BookSumo fans and inspired Karen to pursue her dreams of writing as a career.

*For a complete listing of all my
books please see my author page.*

INTRODUCTION

This book discusses Rock gardening: its types, styles and ways to build a rock garden.

It will explain the concept of rock gardening and why it is important, the book is suitable for both beginners and professionals as well.

It entails techniques and tricks about planning and creating a personal rock garden after introducing the topic to you.

Rock Gardening: A Guide and Inspiration for Creating and Designing Your First Rock Gardens also covers rock plants, their types, names, and colors and the book explains the favorable conditions for their growth.

Most importantly you will receive simple step by step guidelines for creating a rock garden from scratch.

In short, this book is a must for all gardening lovers who desire to learn about rock gardening essentials.

TABLE OF CONTENTS

Contents

Join the VIP Reader List and Get... 2
ABOUT THE AUTHOR. 5
Introduction 7
Table of Contents 9
Any Issues? Contact Me 13
Legal Notes... 14
Chapter 1: What is a Rock Garden? 16
Chapter 2: Types of Rock Gardens 20
    Japanese Rock Garden 20
    American Rock Garden 21
    English Rock Garden 22
    Wall Gardens 23
    Gravel Gardens 24
    Tuck-ins or Alpine Accents 24
Chapter 3: What are Rock Plants? 26
    Considerations to keep in mind 26

Nature of Rock Plants 27

Plants according to their heights 28

   Small-sized rock plants: 28

   Medium-sized rock plants: 28

   Large-sized rock plants: 28

All about Stones and Rocks 29

Chapter 4: Taking Care of your Rock Plants 31

Plan Ahead 31

Prepare A Permanent Place 32

Go for Permanent Solutions 32

Match The Plants With The Site Type 33

Choose Evergreens 33

Suppress Weeds and Others 34

Inspect After Two Weeks 34

Choose Size Of Plants 35

Choose Color Carefully 35

Keep Children Away 35

Winter Care 36

Chapter 5: Best Rock Plants 37

What Are The 10 Best Rock Plants? 37
Catchfly Blooms 37
Thymus Doerfleri 37
Intense Blue/Gentiana Septemfida
 38
Saxifrage 38
Campanula 39
Dwarf Daffodils 39
Delicate Baby's Breath 40
Poached Eggs 40
Dwarf Hardy/Geranium Cinereum
 41
Bugle Call/Ajuga Reptans 41
Chapter 6: Your First Rock Garden 42
Step 1: Clear the Site 43
Step 2: Designing 45
Step 3: Stone Selection 45
Step 4: Boulder Installation 46
Step 5: Adding Plants 46
Step 6: Create a River Illusion 48
Step 7: Plant Setting 49

Step 8: Make Walkways 51

Chapter 7: Ten Tips For a Successful Rock Garden.. 53

    Evaluation of the Site 53

    Drainage 53

    Exposure to the Sunlight................. 53

    Overall Architecture........................ 54

    Effective Use of Plants 54

    Dwarf Planting................................. 55

    Distancing... 55

    Soil and Rocks.................................. 56

    Trough Planting 56

    Narrow-Spaced Rock Gardening..... 57

Join the VIP Reader List and Get... 58

References.. 61

Come On... 69

Let's Be Friends :)............................... 69

About The Publisher............................ 70

Can I Ask A Favour? 71

Interested in Other Gardening Books? 72

ANY ISSUES? CONTACT ME

If you find that something important to you is missing from this book please contact me at karen@booksumo.com.

I will try my best to re-publish a revised copy taking your feedback into consideration and let you know when the book has been revised with you in mind.

:)

— Karen Elliot

Notice to Print Readers:

Hey, because you purchased the print version of this book you are entitled to its original digital version for free by Amazon.

So when you have the time, please review your purchases, and download the Kindle version of this book.

You might enjoy consuming this book more in its original digital format.

;)

But, in any case, take care and enjoy reading in whatever format you choose!

LEGAL NOTES

ALL RIGHTS RESERVED. NO PART OF THIS BOOK MAY BE REPRODUCED OR TRANSMITTED IN ANY FORM OR BY ANY MEANS. PHOTOCOPYING, POSTING ONLINE, AND / OR DIGITAL COPYING IS STRICTLY PROHIBITED UNLESS WRITTEN PERMISSION IS GRANTED BY THE BOOK'S PUBLISHING COMPANY. LIMITED USE OF THE BOOK'S TEXT IS PERMITTED FOR USE IN REVIEWS WRITTEN FOR THE PUBLIC AND/OR PUBLIC DOMAIN.

Chapter 1: What is a Rock Garden?

A rock garden is a garden type that relies on stones and rocks extensively as its main feature along with an amalgam of plants that are native to alpine or rocky areas. Rock gardens are also referred to as Alpine gardens or rockery.

A Zen garden or simply a Japanese rock garden is probably the most famous kind of rock garden which involves only a few plant varieties.

Rock gardens are a well-known feature in landscaping, particularly in tropical areas, some parts of America, Thailand, and Egypt.

Rock gardening is popular in landscape design due to its use of thick shade-producing trees and techniques that prevent excessive plant growth. These are ideal characteristics for both commercial and residential landscaping.

Also a proper rock garden should have no drainage or maintenance issues.

Characteristically, the plants used in Rock gardens are smaller in size such as dwarf trees, perennials, bulbs, and succulents; which are ideally suited to gravelly soil and wobbly outcrops. These plants do not need a lot of water and can survive in drained soil.

These plants can easily grow in troughs, pots, and containers. Being tiny or small, these plants do not overshadow the rocks and stones used throughout the garden.

Therefore, in landscaping, rock gardening is a good solution, when the landscaping area is rugged, inclined, or even hilly. Typically in these same conditions normal gardening is not suitable.

Although there can be many forms, the most common form of rock garden is a heap of multi-shaped rocks, artistically organized together with small plants erupting out from the rock's small breaches.

The most commonly used plant in these gardens are bonsai, though there is a huge variety of plants that can make great rock garden plants such as Pasque flower, Rock soapwort, Seaside flora, stonecrop sedum and Aubretia.

Rock gardens are built to present a natural look to an entire property. Bedding is usually done with stones while plants are used to help in concealing the joints between the stones.

Victorian era rock gardens were designed with this technique. The same technique is applied even today both in commercial and private properties for landscaped rock gardens.

The placement of rocks is in fact one of the most challenging parts in rock gardening because it can either make or mar the overall appeal of the property.

There are a few tricks before starting to work with rocks: begin with the placement of the biggest rock, end with the smallest, and partially bury most rocks at least one third into the soil to offer a more natural appeal.

Lastly, use one rock kind per garden.

In addition, it is also important to plan and place rocks precisely according to the features of the planned garden in your mind because a carelessly planned rock garden will not have a strong appeal to you or visitors.

Make sure, the land has the right amount of soil and drainage before the rocks are placed and before planting is to begin. Once the designing is done, it is very easy to maintain the garden for years as rock gardens do not require a lot of attention and care, except for occasional watering and weeding.

Chapter 2: Types of Rock Gardens

There are three major types of rock gardens which can also be doubly counted as different rock gardening styles. The three are: the Japanese Rock Garden, the American Rock Garden, and the English Rock Garden.

Japanese Rock Garden

The Japanese rock garden which is also called a "Zen or Dry Landscape" garden is the most famous type of rock garden. It features miniature landscapes through the wise selection of composed rock arrangements, moss, water features, sand, gravel, and pruned bushes or trees. Sand is also sometimes used to create various ripple effects in some Japanese rock gardens.

A Japanese rock garden is created in a small place that will typically be surrounded by walls and the location of the garden will have only one viewpoint where it can be seen fully.

AMERICAN ROCK GARDEN

The American rock garden is not as old as the Japanese or English rock garden. The main feature of an American rock garden is its use of any type of plant, tree, or shrub. These plants can be native to the location of the rock garden or they can be completely random.

There are no set requirements for any particular kind of plants which must be used if you would like an American style rock garden. American rock gardening is less traditional and less old fashioned than rock gardening's other two forms.

The North American Rock Garden Society (NARGS) is responsible for expanding the American rock gardening culture among gardeners. NARGS has been propagating the style of American rock gardening since the 1930s and the trend is still expanding.

The American style encourages the easiest and the most suitable way to find small plants, shrubs, perennials, annuals and trees. This style brings innovation in rock gardening because the theme is to use any plant that is available, affordable, or most appealing to the rock gardener.

ENGLISH ROCK GARDEN

The pioneer of Rock gardening in Europe was the English Isle. In the early Victorian period, imported alpine plants could not survive in the English environment due to its difference from the alpine's native environment until around the year 1870.

In 1870 an English gardener wrote a book about rock gardening in which an explanation about alpine plant nature was given to some extent. It helped in building concepts about the theme of rock gardening gradually.

An English rock garden has regulations and rules. These gardens involve layering since the rocks are usually inside the soil.

Layering is typically done gradually and with great care and layering of rocks offered a better environment for the growth of the alpine plant.

This form of layered rock arrangement offered deeper crevices for root growth, while the crowns and tops of the plant could be dry which was crucial to the alpine plant due to the moist English climate.

Apart from regional types, there are also some other types of rock gardens such as: Wall gardens, Gravel gardens and Tuck Ins or Alpine Accents.

WALL GARDENS

As the name suggests, wall gardens are all about rock gardening on the walls. There are two basic kinds of walls: Dry and Mortared.

Dry walls are stony walls that are cautiously arranged for interlocking with each other. Mortared walls on the other hand, are made up of concrete, stones or bricks and have gaps that are filled with cement for increased strength.

Gravel Gardens

In gravel or scree gardens, garden soil is amended for boosting drainage; a gravel garden requires gravel, peat moss, or coarse sand of up to six inches.

Scree is another name for this type of garden. Scree gardens occur naturally when rocks from hilly areas form gravel after erosion. This erosion gives birth to natural gravel gardens. Plants that make good gravel garden plants include Dwarf Conifers and Jeeper Creepers.

Tuck-ins or Alpine Accents

Alpine accents are also known as tuck-ins because they are used to decorate the empty or vacant corners of the garden, for instance, beside a walkway, along the patio or on the flagstone stepping. They make good borders or edges.

Chapter 3: What are Rock Plants?

By definition, rock plants are plants which can grow on or between rocks. Most rock plants share some common characteristics such as being tiny and tough, they require good drainage, and they grow more effectively in slanted areas. Therefore, ideal placement for rock plants is on the rear or side of a property.

It is usually necessary to plant more than one species in the garden because typically rock gardens contain more than one type of plant but for an American style rock garden one type of plant is okay.

Considerations to keep in mind

Always plan before selecting plants for your rock garden; this plan should include the following things: a detailed outline of plant maintenance requirements, notation of the climatic conditions of the gardening area, and note the land type and terrain features of the gardening area. Always try to plant in sunnier places.

Be careful when planting shrubs because they expand quickly and hence not all shrubs are favorable for a compact garden. Do group plants for highlighting their attraction. Use only miniature conifers as other types do not make better rock plants.

NATURE OF ROCK PLANTS

Rock plants are slow growing by nature and tend to form clumps. They prefer well drained soil and grow steadily if the favorable atmosphere is provided to them. The most commonly preferred rock plants include: perennials, evergreens, and some types of annuals.

Plants according to their heights

Rock plants are majorly considered to be tiny plants. But the fact is, not all tiny plants will make good rock plants plus it is also not necessary that all rock plants are tiny. They come in three main sizes: small, medium and large.

Small-sized rock plants:

Creeping Thyme, Blue Fescue, Ajuga, Candytuft, Purple Ice plant, Hens and Chicks, Chocolate Chip, Burgundy Glow and Yellow Alyssum, and Dragon's Blood.

Medium-sized rock plants:

Lavender, Yarrow, Black-eyed Susan, Shashta Daisy, Columbine, Basket of gold, Blue Bell, Yellow Sulfur, Blue Rug juniper, Six hills Giant catmint, Miss Willmott, and Compactum.

Large-sized rock plants:

Russian sage, Firefly Coral Bells, Lamb's ear, Mugo pine, Rock spray cotoneaster, and Avalanche.

ALL ABOUT STONES AND ROCKS

Rocks are an integral part of a rock garden. It is recommended to use native rocks and stones since they are easy to obtain and low in cost.

Outsized and irregular shaped rocks offer an interesting appeal in rock gardens. However, miniature rocks also play a huge role as well.

Limestone is a great choice in rock gardening as it is soft and contains pores which allow water to pass through it. Limestone typically contains several depressions in it which can be filled up for planting purposes. Start working from the lowest slope to the highest position in the rock garden. For firmness, shovel a heap of soil around the rock and spray water afterwards.

Soil will take a few days to settle down. Wait for some days and do not start planting unless the rock layout looks appealing and the soil has settled.

Weathered stones are a good substitute to limestone. Granite on the other hand, is not recommended as it is a dense rock that dries up very quickly. Do not use un-weathered sandstone and scaly rocks.

River rocks and tawny pebbles are used to add color and contrast to the garden. They symbolize warmth; white marble also creates a brightening effect.

Large uniquely-shaped boulders can become a center of attraction in the garden, giving eyes an exotic sensation.

In choosing rocks, try to be as natural as possible. They should be in harmony with the overall feel of the area. Be uniform by adding only one kind of rock and stone in the rock garden as it creates a subconscious rhythm.

Chapter 4: Taking Care of your Rock Plants

Care comes first when talking about rock plants because without adequate care the aesthetic rock garden will turn into a secluded, desert-like area and all your hard work will be spoiled. Therefore, to shun such possibilities, rock plant care is the most essential thing for all gardeners from day one.

Unlike other garden plants, rock plants do not need extensive attention. There is only one basic rule, plan attentively and relax for the rest of the time because an attentively planned rock garden does not require daily attention.

Plan Ahead

As already mentioned, designing is quite challenging and cannot be handled without having a good creative ability and imaginative power to foresee how the rockery will look after putting in effort to build it. Therefore, it is essential to sketch the design in your mind first while keeping the natural features of the place in mind.

Prepare for an effective drainage route by mixing six to seven inches of rubble, broken bricks, gravel, coarse sand and pea shingle in the planting area. This will be helpful in draining the water well, and remember rock plants typically require good draining.

Prepare A Permanent Place

Unlike landscaping, it is not easy to transfer rock plants from one place to the other, so find a place that is permanent and secluded which means there should be no pipelines or other disturbing things under or above the soil.

Go for Permanent Solutions

Always go for permanent solutions especially in the case of rock planting as it cannot be done time and again. For example, if the soil is not weed resistant, add a horticulture weed resistant fabric or two layers of old newspaper in the base. Add compost and manure occasionally for enhancing soil quality. But ideally fertilization of the area should be performed a few months before you begin planting.

Match The Plants With The Site Type

This is perhaps the most important thing in rock plant care that will keep problems at bay. If a warm climate based plant is planted in cooler northern region, it will surely not be able to grow well, unless proper planning has been done for it. Keep soil and plant types in mind. If you match your plants to your locality the maintenance that you will need to perform will be much less.

Choose Evergreens

Evergreens are considered as a backbone in rock gardens because the overall appeal of the garden can depend upon them. Choose sedums and alpines as they go great with rocks. Some examples of alpines are: some kinds Penstemons, Picea, Dianthus and Celmisia Ramulosa.

SUPPRESS WEEDS AND OTHERS

Suppress weeds and other unwanted pop ups by involving weed suppressers into your plan. They have double functions: they decrease weed growth and they add value to the garden. Common weed suppressors are Creeping Sedums and Leptinella potentillina.

INSPECT AFTER TWO WEEKS

Although rock plants are low maintenance and can survive without daily attention this does not mean you can neglect them completely.

It is crucial to check on the plants at least every two weeks. Examine weed growth, check for ants and other pests, and assess general health and growth.

For ants, use a borax, water, and sugar mixture, particularly between crevices of the stones or rocks. It is good to loosen all the areas of plants with a small fork after three months. Spend two hours per week in staking, deadheading and cleaning debris.

CHOOSE SIZE OF PLANTS

When planting, it is recommended to choose the right size for the right rock. This means always choose larger sized plants for larger rocks and smaller for smaller rocks. Plants are meant to enhance the beauty of the rock, not hide it.

CHOOSE COLOR CAREFULLY

Keep in mind to choose contrasting or complimenting colors of the plants with the rocks. Otherwise, the color of the rock will overshadow the plant's color.

KEEP CHILDREN AWAY

Being tiny and small in size, rock plants are more prone to being stepped on or plucked accidently.

Make sure they are planted in a safe place where human activities will not destroy them, particularly, children should be warmed about harming the plant unintentionally.

Winter Care

Remove all dying leaves in autumn and trim your plant's stems because leaving this job for spring will harm the plant. Envelop all sensitive plants in the winter and during spring renew feed and mulch after the first frost.

Chapter 5: Best Rock Plants

What Are The 10 Best Rock Plants?

The varieties of rock plants are limitless. But the best plants are those which are easy to cultivate, easy to adjust and available everywhere.

Catchfly Blooms

Catchfly or Campion is a vibrant perennial that makes an ideal rock plant. It offers a silvery foliage with a long color range that starts from red to white and rose pink. It is used in large quantities for making borders, though it can also grow in pots or containers. It prefers a well drained, humid site.

Thymus Doerfleri

Thyme Bressingham pink or simply "Thymus Doerfleri" offers evergreen flowers with appealing foliage. This plant resists drought and is also a valuable kitchen herb. It can be planted in containers, can be carpeted or used in edging. Its height is no more than six inches.

Intense Blue/Gentiana Septemfida

Gentiana septemfida is commonly known as "Intense blue" because of its brilliant blue blossoms. They are low growing plants and work well when grown on the walls, between the rock crevices or in pots. Its size is no more than 20 cm and it originates from Turkey and Caucasus. It works well in drained and moist soil. It requires full sun exposure.

Saxifrage

Saxifrage sancta are an evergreen alpine that produce yellow flowers during late spring or in the beginning of the summers. They need direct sun exposure and an average water level to grow well. Its maximum height is 10 cm.

Campanula

Campanula, purple stars, or bell flower, come in many forms, shapes, sizes, and shades. The blooming season of this plant is early spring to summer and it bears blue, white, or pink colored flowers.

They make great borders and can also be grown on small cliffs. Campanula grows from 6 inches to 3 feet. It is a low maintenance and drought tolerant perennial. They can even grow in partial sunlight.

Dwarf Daffodils

Dwarf Daffodils are commonly known as Tete-a-Tete. They are usually used in edging or bordering because of their clustered growth.

Dwarf Daffodils bear beautiful golden colored flowers in the spring season. Their stems can bear three blooms.

Their maximum height is not more than 15 cm. and they grow well both under sun and shade.

Delicate Baby's Breath

Baby's birth is a well-known plant that bears light sprays of light pink blooms. They make excellent borders and are capable of covering the ground wonderfully. Well drained soil and good sunlight is what it requires. Their maximum height is about 30 inches.

Poached Eggs

The poached egg plant, also known as "Limnanthes douglasii", is an annual that makes an ideal rock plant because they can adapt to almost any type of soil that is under a sunny place.

Their vibrant cup shaped yellow and white flowers make a great patch on the ground. It is an independent plant that germinates and naturalizes itself. It is six to twelve inches in height typically.

Dwarf Hardy/Geranium Cinereum

Geranium cinereum or Dwarf Hardy Geranium is a dwarf perennial which contains big lilac pink flowers with grayish green leaves.

Dwarf Hardy requires full sun exposure with well-drained soil. Its maximum height is 4 to 6 inches. They flower in late springs.

Bugle Call/Ajuga Reptans

Ajuga reptans, also known as "Bugle Call", is a multi-colored bugleweed.

It is an excellent ground carpet that contains bronze colored leaves with pink and cream colored borders.

It is a fast growing plant with bluish-purple flowers. It grows 4 to 14 inches in height.

Chapter 6: Your First Rock Garden

Beginning your first rock gardening is both exciting and exhausting because it will require a lot of energy and effort to create a successful plan. Rock gardening is not the easiest form of gardening but a careful gardener can succeed in it.

After planning and choosing the site, it is essential to gather materials that are needed this will typically include: mulch, crushed limestone, flowers, peat moss, fertilizer, marking paint, flagstones and plants.

Make sure you have the following tools ready and available: hoe, shears, rake, crowbar, edger, shovel, wheelbarrow and leaf blower.

Below is a step by step guide to create your first rock garden.

But note that, it is crucial to keep time in mind. Spring is the best season to create a rock garden since a plethora of plants will be available during that time.

Autumn and early winter is for building and designing the garden's main features because less hard work will involved during this time given you will not be planting.

You want to try and avoid beginning your rock garden around times of severe weather, typically months like September as the severity in weather which will adversely affect the plants.

Step 1: Clear the Site

The first step is clearance of the site. Bushes, brush, unwanted grass, and all undergrowth should be removed with the help of a leaf blower or rake.

With the help of a shovel, dig all of the bushes out of the ground along with their roots to avoid any future growth.

Use a pair of shears for cutting larger sized plants and use a hoe for tiny plants, extra stems, branches or vegetation.

After completing this step, create the required shape for adding mulch, stones and plants. The objective should be to highlight the surrounding area by creating a border or edge with the help of an edger.

The edge should be deep enough that extra, unwashed mulch and stone can be settled in it without disturbing the overall design/shape of the lawn.

Note: Always try to choose the most favorable site one that is away from trees, has maximum sun exposure, and there is nothing to overshadow the rock garden.

Direct sunlight for a few hours of the day is more preferable than 12 hours of indirect light received in a shady place. For soil with bad drainage, involve some grit.

Step 2: Designing

In step two, a bit of a landscaping is needed. Take inverted marking paint and start marking the required style that you have created. Check for its flow and harmony with the overall shape of the lawn. You are marking the location of things in your design.

Step 3: Stone Selection

Select required stones and boulders. Involve a variety of sizes with small and large boulders of the same type, flagstones, and possibly colorful river bed stones and flat stones for walkways.

A quarry can be hired to deliver the required stone list. Notice the weight of small and large stones. They range from 100 pounds to 500 pounds. Therefore, be careful while working with them.

Note: Choose according to the design requirements. Do you want the rock garden to be the center of attention in your lawn? If so maybe you will need a few more large stones.

Step 4: Boulder Installation

It is recommended to start with the heaviest stone. Therefore, set the boulders at first. Roll them into place by using stone shims and crowbars. Make a footing for fixing the boulders so they appear natural and well placed.

For boulders, it is essential to know that they should be buried into the soil (at least a few inches), placed permanently, and be made immobile.

A boulder sitting on the top of the ground will tend to look both unnatural and possibly artificial. Also they will be more prone to movement in the case of strong winds or storms.

Step 5: Adding Plants

Add plants that are most suitable to the native environment. There should be a blend of different colors and textures which should boost the general appeal of the garden.

There are a myriad of plants that can be used in the garden including: annuals, perennials, alpines, tiny shrubs, dwarf conifers and evergreens etc. Always go for the plants that flower year round, make mats on ground and possibly choose plants which are tiny in size. Consult my list of the top 10 best and most beautiful rock plants in chapter 5 if you have not already.

For example, Hostas or Dog's-tooth violet (*Erythronium*), Ivy, Hardy ferns and Violas make a great group in a rock garden. Or Daphne cneorum, Euphorbia myrsinites, and Iberis sempervirens can be applied as another option.

Note: It is suggested to check a nursery catalog before buying plants. However some of the best looking gardens involve the use of Chrysanthemums with Rugged juniper, Portulaca with

California poppies, Dwarf Daffodils and Saxifrage together in the site.

Step 6: Create a River Illusion

Although this is not required it can be a brilliant idea to create a river illusion with the use of mini boulders, junipers and river stones.

Begin by placing junipers at the highest point of the rock garden's area.

Use peat moss along with fertilizer when planting junipers; as the peat will help in holding water, while fertilizer will be its food.

Dig a water bed in a straight line after planting the junipers. Arrange tiny boulders along the bed for producing the illusion.

The arrangement should not be formal and should have a footing.

Add small river bed stones, but to keep weeds away, lay anti-weed fabric or spray weed control first before placing any river bed stones.

Note: The right process to arranging stones is to place the larger stones as a base, while placing smaller stones on top. Angle all rocks and stones in such a way that rain water would run off of them.

STEP 7: PLANT SETTING

After the creation of the river illusion (or before it, if you choose to not create an illusion), continue setting desired plants. Try to create some unique but natural designs in your plant arrangements.

Play with different shades and textures and mingle them together. Spread flowers everywhere so they offer a spectacular appeal. Use potted plants as well. Adjust them to the desired place.

This step takes the most of time since all the hard work and attraction of the garden is dependent upon the final placement of your plants, so be careful in designing and setting your plants.

Grouping is great but group similar looking flowers, or set groups of flowers whose colors are complementary. Your mantra in setting your final groups of plants should be innovation, variety, and uniqueness.

In the case of container plants, loosen their roots first after taking them out of the container. Expose their fibers a bit so that they can seep water quickly after getting adjusted in the soil.

Dig plant holes wider than the roots. The plants should not be too deep burry them so that about 75% of the plant is covered and a quarter of the top is free.

Add mulch while planting and make sure that the roots of your plant will be able to absorb water properly.

Note: Try to understand the position of plants in pots before setting them into the soil.

This will help you in previewing their required position. This enables you to see which position suits them the most. In the case of working between the crevices, add compost with mulch to seal moisture in and keep weed growth minimal.

STEP 8: MAKE WALKWAYS

Finally, make the walkway by setting the walking stones. Walkways are made both to walk on and to enhance the focal point of the rock garden. Follow the design by placing the stones in their position. For this purpose, use a shovel for tracing a stone's position, remove extra rocks and stones and make a footing. And fix the stone in it.

In order to boost the beauty of the garden, involve bed stones in between the walkways by using a shovel. Try to add a calculated amount instead of overdoing it since an overdone walkway lacks attractiveness.

Now, add some mulch which is basically used for decoration, weed protection and water retention.

With hard work and imagination your rock garden will now be set to grow and amaze all who view it.

Note: It is important to note that the maximum time it should take to follow this plan and create a rock garden is about 48 to 60 hours.

Chapter 7: Ten Tips for a Successful Rock Garden

Evaluation of the Site

Site evaluation is the first tip for becoming a successful rock gardener. Critically analyze the place that is to be designed and take note of its overall architecture, exposure to sunlight, and the availability of natural rocks and stones within the place.

Drainage

Drainage comes second in rock gardening. Raised sites, slopes, and slants are a good choice in designing because inclined sites are better drained than others and a well-drained site is an important requirement for most rock plants.

Exposure to the Sunlight

Sunlight exposure is also an essential requirement in rock gardening because most rock plants grow well in the presence of sunlight. Do not plan to create your rock garden in a shady location.

Overall Architecture

It is crucial that the design of the rock garden and the overall architecture must match with each other for creating harmony and an aesthetic appeal about the place in general.

A large rock, a stone wall, and some bricks will help in creating a natural appeal to the overall design of the rock garden. It also creates a focal point which will be worth paying attention to.

Therefore, your design should try to remain as natural as possible because an artificial looking rock garden does not appeal most people.

Effective Use of Plants

Different types of plants create different types of sensations. A rock garden should contain a nice and well defined proportion of colors and blends that will produce a soothing and relaxing effect on the property owners.

For this reason, plant selection should be strict and careful because a careless combination could mar the overall impact of the garden.

For selecting plants, also remember to choose similar natural plants and visualize their color contrast beforehand.

Dwarf Planting

The dwarf plant types should be grown in containers because growing them in the ground will hide their beauty.

Distancing

Given that rock plants are typically smaller in size and cannot grow tall enough to disturb or overshadow a building's appearance, it is recommended to plant them near entrances or near walkways.

SOIL AND ROCKS

It is easy to control soil because rock planting typically involves imported soil. With a little manipulation it is possible to grow a rock garden in a congested place, on a wall, or in narrow crevices by involving porous stones.

Rocks should be natural in appearance and porous as discussed before. Typical rock garden stones are salvaged rocks, sandstone, limestone, and granite.

Sandstone is an ideal rock because it is neither too hard nor too dense and it is widely obtainable as well.

TROUGH PLANTING

Remember that you can also grow plants in containers and troughs and place them throughout the rock garden strategically for added colors and greater mass appeal.

NARROW-SPACED ROCK GARDENING

Alpines can create great miniature art which can be applied in narrow-spaced gardening because alpines can grow easily in small pots and containers.

These containers or pots can be used to decorate the balconies, narrow side yards, patios and even room windows of a house if not used in your rock garden.

JOIN THE VIP READER LIST AND GET...

Send the Book!

Join my private mailing list of readers and get a copy of my book: ***Garden Ideas: An Introduction to Different Gardening Types and Methods* for FREE*!***

In this book I introduce many of the gardening methods you've heard of, but may not fully understand. We will discuss: *container gardening, lasagna gardening, heirloom organic gardens, water gardening, bonsai's, straw bale gardening, and others!*

Learn about the different gardening methods available! This book is not available anywhere else and is only for my private list of readers!

You will also receive updates about all my new books when they are free. So please show your support.

Also don't forget to like and subscribe on the social networks. I love meeting my readers. Links to all my profiles are below so please click and connect :)

Facebook

Twitter

Google +

REFERENCES

"All about Rock Gardens." *All about Rock Gardens*. Rock Star Plants.com, n.d. Web. 16 June 2015. <http://www.rockstarplants.com/about.html>.

"Bellflower." *Better Homes & Gardens*. N.p., n.d. Web. 16 June 2015. <http://www.bhg.com/gardening/plant-dictionary/perennial/bellflower/>.

"The Best Plants For Rock Gardens | Plants for Rocky Soil : HGTV Gardens." *HGTVGardens*. N.p., n.d. Web. 16 June 2015. <http://www.hgtvgardens.com/flowers-and-plants/the-best-plants-for-rock-gardens>.

"Campion, Catchfly." *HGTV*. N.p., n.d. Web. 16 June 2015. <http://www.hgtv.com/design/outdoor-design/landscaping-and-hardscaping/campion-catchfly>.

"Designing a Rock Garden." *Planttalk Colorado*. Colorado State University, n.d. Web. 16 June 2015. <http://www.ext.colostate.edu/ptlk/1115.html>.

"Good Rock Garden Plants." *Rock Garden Plants - NARGS*. North American Rock Garden Society, n.d. Web. <https%3A%2F%2Fwww.nargs.org%2Freference%2Fgood-rock-garden-plants>.

"Ground Covers and Rock Garden Plants for Mountain Communities." *Ground Covers and Rock Garden Plants for Mountain Communities*. N.p., n.d. Web. 16 June 2015. <http://www.ext.colostate.edu/pubs/garden/07413.html>.

"How to Care for a Rock Garden - HowStuffWorks." *HowStuffWorks*. N.p., n.d. Web. 16 June 2015. <http://home.howstuffworks.com/gardening/garden-trends/how-to-plan-a-rock-garden3.htm>.

"How to Make a Rock Garden." *DIY*. N.p., n.d. Web. 16 June 2015. <http://www.diynetwork.com/how-to/outdoors/gardening/how-to-make-a-rock-garden>.

"Intro to Rock Gardening." *NRGS*. North American Rock Gardening Society, n.d. Web. 16 June 2015. <https%3A%2F%2Fwww.nargs.org%2Freference%2Fintro-rock-gardening>.

"Make a Shady Rock Garden." *HGTV*. N.p., n.d. Web. 16 June 2015. <http://www.hgtv.com/design/outdoor-design/landscaping-and-hardscaping/make-a-shady-rock-garden>.

"Narcissus 'Tete-a-Tete'" - *Daffodil Bulbs*. N.p., n.d. Web. 16 June 2015. <http://www.thompson-morgan.com/flowers/flower-bulbs/daffodil-bulbs/narcissus-tete-a-tete/t46039TM>.

"Planting a Rock Garden - Plants For Rock Gardens : HGTV Gardens." *HGTVGardens*. N.p., 12 Jan. 2013. Web. 16 June 2015. <http://www.hgtvgardens.com/garden-types/tips-for-planting-a-rock-garden>.

"Rock Garden Design Tips, 15 Rocks Garden Landscape Ideas." *Lushome*. N.p., n.d. Web. 16 June 2015. <http://www.lushome.com/rock-garden-design-tips-15-rocks-garden-landscape-ideas/76475>.

"Rock Garden." *Rock Garden*. N.p., n.d. Web. 16 June 2015. <http://www.susansgardenpatch.com/rock20.htm>.

"Rock Gardening." *RHS Gardening*. N.p., n.d. Web. 16 June 2015. <https://www.rhs.org.uk/advice/profile?pid=837>.

"Rock Gardening Tips for Small Spaces." *Rock Gardening Tips for Small Spaces*. N.p., n.d. Web. 16 June 2015. <http://www.flower-gardening-made-easy.com/rock-gardening-tips.html>.

"Rock Gardens, Creating and Caring for Rock Gardens." *Rock Gardens, Creating and Caring for Rock Gardens*. Gardeners Network, n.d. Web. 16 June 2015. <http://www.gardenersnet.com/gardening/rockgardens.htm>.

"Rock Gardens." *GardenGuides*. N.p., n.d. Web. 16 June 2015.

<http://www.gardenguides.com/593-rock-gardens.html>.

"Rock Gardens." *Sheridan Nurseries*. Sheridan Nurseries, n.d. Web. 16 June 2015. <http://www.sheridannurseries.com/garden_tips/general_gardening/rock_gardens>.

"Rock Gardens." *Wikipedia*. Wikimedia Foundation, n.d. Web. 16 June 2015. <http://en.wikipedia.org/wiki/Garden_design#Rock_garden>.

"Selecting Plants for a Rock Garden." *Space for Life*. N.p., n.d. Web. 16 June 2015. <http://espacepourlavie.ca/en/selecting-plants-rock-garden>.

"Wall Gardens." *Rock Stars®*. Rock Star Plants.com, n.d. Web. 16 June 2015. <http://www.rockstarplants.com/wallgardens.html>.

Come On...
Let's Be Friends :)

I adore my readers and love connecting with them socially. Please follow the links below so we can connect on Facebook, Twitter, and Google+.

Facebook

Twitter

Google +

I also have a blog that I regularly update for my readers so check it out below.

My Blog

ABOUT THE PUBLISHER.

BookSumo specializes in providing the best books on special topics that you care about. *Rock Gardens: A Guide and Inspiration for Creating and Designing Your First Rock Garden* is everything you ever wanted to know about this unique type of garden.

To find out more about BookSumo and find other books we have written go to: http://booksumo.com/.

CAN I ASK A FAVOUR?

If you found this book interesting, or have otherwise found any benefit in it. Then may I ask that you post a review of it on Amazon? Nothing excites me more than new reviews, especially reviews which suggest new topics for writing. I do read all reviews and I always factor feedback into my newer works.

So if you are willing to take ten minutes to write what you sincerely thought about this book then please visit our Amazon page and post your opinions.

Again thank you!

INTERESTED IN OTHER GARDENING BOOKS?

Check out all my gardening books at my Amazon author page:

For a complete listing of all my books please see my author page.

Printed in Great Britain
by Amazon